FARM

FARM

Marilyn Cay

Thistledown Press Ltd.

Canadian Cataloguing in Publication Data
Cay, Marilyn,

Farm

(New leaf editions)
Poems
ISBN 1-895449-12-X

I. Title. II. Series.

PS8555.A898F3 1993 C811'.54 C93-098145-6
PR9199.3.C389F3 1993

Book design by A.M. Forrie
Cover art by Stevi Kittleson
Typeset by Thistledown Press Ltd.

Printed and bound in Canada by
Kromar Printing Ltd.
725 Portage Ave.
Winnipeg, MB R3G 0M8

Thistledown Press Ltd.
668 East Place
Saskatoon, Saskatchewan S7J 2Z5

Acknowledgements:

Poems in this collection have appeared previously in *200% Cracked Wheat, Prairie Dreams, Heading Out, From Seedbed to Harvest, Western People, Cross Canada Writer's Magazine, Canadian Author and Bookman, NeWest Review, Grain*, and in the chapbook *Pure and Startled Seconds*. Selections were aired on "Ambience", CBC.

Special thanks to Susan Andrews Grace for her steady encouragement and good advice, and to Paulette Jiles, Fort San, 1987, Sharon Thesen, Sage Hills, 1990 and members of the Tisdale Writers Group.

This book has been published with the assistance of The Canada Council and the Saskatchewan Arts Board.

to my husband
Norman

CONTENTS

1. FARM WOMAN

2. PURE AND STARTLED SECONDS

3. FARM

4. STILL LIFES

. . .Getting and spending, we lay waste our powers:
Little we see in Nature that is ours;
We have given our hearts away, . . .
William Wordsworth

farm woman

she drinks cold coffee
and eats half a dirty cookie
while the truck dumps, she
rinses barley dust from her back at midnight
makes sandwiches and

paints red polish on her toes while fresh coffee perks
and augers swirl grain
in the dark

a farm woman paints herself
into a picture, a spring scene
by a creek
she paints from memory the feel
of cool putty mud
oozing between her toes and the way
lime green poplar leaves tremble
squares of diamond sunlight

suddenly
she must leave her perfect feet
sever them in shallow water
and rush to town for supplies
she paints quicker, her body
arches in a pickup truck, she
blurs the wheels to show haste
and wipes a streak of white
to catch the gas barrel that slides across the box
dust trails her out of the picture

just after noon she returns to her canvas
and paints her arm in the foreground
with an ant squashed on it
this is to remember
she murdered an innocent insect
for intruding upon her moment
alone

a wasted day

to Lily, 1889

she must have wasted the whole day
painting that collie, his handsome face
close up, nose looking cold to the touch
I wonder what bread or pie
she didn't bake, which floor
that went unswept, who will ever know now
while she fooled with paint and canvas
her family probably had to wash their hands
in a basin with a ring around it
maybe she didn't even carry fresh water, maybe
they had to wash in grey water
left over from morning, while
she fevered herself
with that painting
the one of the dog
that still hangs

passing through

for Gordon Lightfoot

that plastic disc is thick looking now
dark and scarred
a long time has passed since it was new
we were young
we would strum on winter nights
trying to get it like Gord
I could only chord but you
had sheet music and practised picking
you planned to own a Framus guitar
some day, and live near pines and a lake

sometimes
I put the needle down and listen
to those Don Quixote lines
I shut my eyes as the horseman passes
see his hand reach into the saddlebag
and scatter dreams
I go back on memories
of long hair and bell-bottom jeans
everything was so fine
in 1969

you will explore the perimeters of your pasture
this day, as I will
trotting head high, nostrils wide
seeking the fallen wire
the broken post
the weak place

running
until wind rasps our throats
and hearts pound louder than hooves

I will watch us in the evening
as the sun sets and shadows cool our hot brows

by the big tree in the meadow
heads down
manes wet along our necks
closeness against the universe

stains

a woman is exhausted
from sharing household hints all day
a booth in the mall, she has an answer
for everything, rust on the bathtub
stains on the sheets

pain taps her eyebrows
she touches them and pulls
on the round collar of her cute dress
        that other woman
all day in the store, across
from the stain display
staring and smoking, dark eyes amused
pencil skirt, slits, slender bare legs
the way men stared at her
while their wives were lost
to soda and vinegar, ammonia
and salt

sometimes silence
is like warm salve
flowing around hurts, fluid
from body heat

today your silence
is liquid blackness and cool
a brush dips methodically
the artist painting dark spaces
around my shoulders and face
I see myself
as lost light
features formless
against shadows

far away
on a lake I imagine cool and blue
you dip your paddle
and aim your canoe across the languid water
to where the river sneaks away
and rushes to the rapids

men do this
drive hundreds of miles in hot trucks
carry canoes and supplies over bush trails
sleep in two-man tents
and dip their bare bums in ice water
when morning comes
man stuff

the rapids are inside my mind
they fall and tumble periodically
I see you bobbing at the water's whim
I know you are testing yourself
I have confidence you will win the day
my canoe is a couch and it is comfortable
I think of you
during the commercials

sisters in time

each year our machines
rearrange the relics
rain lashes the hillside
and one day a scarred scraper
washes up clean and
pulls my hand toward it

through your tepee flap
poplar smoke rises
iskwew woman
I am a strange vision in your dreams
for seconds
I see the muscles in your brown arms
as you ply the pelts
my fingers feel the roughness
curl around the edges
as if it was mine

sister of time
life is more tangible than visions
but the wind is your leather skirt
parting the grass
where I pass

1.
a middle aged farm woman tries to enter a conversation
she says *remember the field of roots*
I picked that summer?
it was so hot
that was the year I made all those pickles too
the year I was pregnant with Nancy
or Donnie or Floyd or Meggie

but the men and children
are anxious to get back to what they were saying

2.
as an old woman she corners a minister
on a street in town
talking loudly, quickly, and crying
I canned seventy-nine quarts of saskatoons
and he never even noticed
he never even noticed
he never even noticed

my mother could have been
a movie star, she was so pretty
but a girl didn't go to Hollywood
during the great depression
she went to work on a farm
and married the farmer
and milked cows and had babies
and became the best raisin pie maker
on earth

she had long dark hair
that she wished was red
like Susan Hayward's
Mom would toss her head in the sun
and ask if we could see
red in her hair
sometimes my brother and I
would tell her we could see it

Dad was never too busy
to take her to Susan Hayward movies
my brother and I thought it was ridiculous
what he went through
when *The Snows of Kilimanjaro* came to town
he had to pull the car with the tractor
the roads were so muddy
we'd go in spite of anything

faces

in the 50s
my dad shaved once a week, in fact
at noons he didn't even wash his face
and when I'd ask him why not
he'd say he wasn't using his face
I'd try to think of how
a person could use a face

on Saturday nights
he'd take out the old chipped china cup
and slap the lather up
with his hog bristle brush
the blue blade slipped through
snipping his orange whiskers
I'd watch them floating in the basin

Dad's face would be smooth as taffeta
through most of Sunday

rituals

a farm man
splashes his face at the sink
cheeks bulged
lips pursed, spurting and blowing
like a tired dusty elephant

the water lies
in grey slimy pools around the taps
more often than not
with a fly spinning to death in it

his wife flaps her ears, lifts her trunk
and blasts him, *don't*
spray the water like that!
but he does it anyway
as if it is his privilege

coming of age

we were fourteen years old
at our first dance
in the old country hall
we raced through darkness outside
giddy on the coolness of night air
our skirts flew, the sharp-netted crinolines
pricked at our legs

past a car
parked right by the step
bare limbs protruding, white
in the glare from the hall door
neither one of us spoke

beer reeked from the stag line
we snaked our way through
heading for the wallflower seats
we laughed as if no one
could have as much fun

it's a simple manoeuvre
slipping through the strands of barbed wire
but the sun plays tricks on me, scattering light
flashing it in patches from tall poplars
instead of stepping into my pasture
I pass into my grandfather's yard
down the hill from the house at the wire gate
where Prince, the big bay horse
came to stand in the evenings
my grandfather is there with a handful of oats
the horse's big lips twitch on his palm
he strokes the horse along his damp neck
under oily tangles of mane
then he pulls aside the wire gate
and catches Prince's firm dimpled bottom lip
and leads him to the water trough
the horse drinks and grandfather
collects the rim of drops
from the horse's mouth on his hand
and wipes his hand on his pants

was it the light?
the way it danced on the ground?
all I truly remember is Prince
standing alone at the wire gate

a woman has fear on her brow
at her husband's oldness
his last days

she has pummelled him with silence
with words
neither effective
against his dirty boots
all those years on the farm

she would never bring it up again
if only he could live a little longer

words collect
blue robin eggs in my nest heart
all winter
incubating
I find them in the garden
in May
near the apple tree
empty halves
gaping at the sky

my son
is learning to drive
he is careful at first
then spins on ice
and finds it thrilling
he laughs

at night I dream
I am slapping him
I will make him understand
I strike him until
the small bones in my hands break
his face does not redden
and he keeps smiling
I do not know if he
felt it at all

a pure and startled second

to my son

I want to phone the high school
and have you paged out of the classroom
as if there is an emergency
I want to hear the clumping sound
of your feet, running down the hall
    your hand on the receiver
      my voice to your ear
        I love you

before the rush of teenage anger
the cynical, the cruel rebuff
there is a pure and startled second
it is this second I want from you

I'll hang up quickly then
before you can hurt me

in the pocket of her son's jeans

a woman's headache
is in the pocket of her son's jeans
along with other minor interruptions
in his life
a warning from the cops, his report card
the bill for fixing his stereo
some change and his lighter
things, far from his centre, where he is king
and god almighty
he dumps it all on his dresser
at 2 a.m., kicks the jeans in the corner
they need washing
he sleeps
long and lean
his mouth open

pride

he challenges his father
to arm wrestle
and the two ready themselves
at the kitchen table
this time
there is something about the son's calmness
that makes the father insist upon a fair start
his arm tense
the father breaks with speed
in order to put his son's arm down soundly

but he meets with iron this time
the two arms tremble, straight up and down
muscles bulging
hands gripping tightly

afterwards the mother says
the father was the big winner
even though it is her son
whose strength prevailed

you face me with bleeding gums
    frightened
your quest for beauty
made you sit the chair
you let them pull the four teeth
you, who cannot stand a sliver
picked from your finger

I'll take you home
and soothe your brow
with cool water
and work quietly while you sleep
    your mouth parted
silver braces tugging
teeth into spaces
someday you will smile
with no hands

to daughter

it's cliche but
your eyes really are like cornflowers
so blue and round
your smile angelic
I don't know why you resisted my mothering
never fit
my opinions

I crumpled your ideas
like papers, now
that you're gone
I dig them out of the waste can
cast them across my table
finger them
and think they are valid

the day we picked the apartment

I didn't cry
I fought the feeling back
        through the ladies' wear
        through the childrens' section
of the store
until deep inside the dirty bathroom
    there
in the pungency of other womens' smells
sitting flat out on the seat, mindless
of germ armies
the tears flowed
face in hands

my daughter waited outside
I could see her through the crack
in those seconds when I lifted my eyes
she lounged against the sink
what a big deal
picking her first apartment

the road

for Karen

outside this yard
with its house and light, is the whole world
and you are in it, driving
somewhere through the dark night

aurora borealis hangs
the lawn grass is wet and cold
beyond this, the laneway leads to the road
and that road to all roads

you are a set of headlights
bright upon the darkness
and I trust the road that leads away
comes back again

when you come home you still
bring food into the living room
and cut your toenails
while watching TV, leaving
the white discs on the couch
and your damp towel drapes across the rocking chair
two things have changed
    I am speechless
    and you will soon leave

in the living room after you are gone
the furnace blows heat under the drapes
        they billow
        they droop
on television
a woman is running into winter
I hold on to the chair arms
and hold myself back

through a hole that cannot be unmade

a woman throws a cup
with the strength of a ball player overhand
she is amazed at the spontaneity
the power

the cup is pink is plastic is unbreakable

it seems this is happening
because the boy left the door open again
let flies in
she wonders about the white wall

was it her fortieth birthday last week
the wind
trying to get into the house the cashier
at the grocery store earlier that day insulting
the old man?

the unbreakable pink plastic
cup shatters
splits
jagged pieces fly
some back to her
some into the universe
through a hole
that cannot be unmade

April begins with a promise
of summer, soon broken
mangy snow horses bear down heavily
whipped by a north wind
they pound into pastures on chipped hooves
they have come to murder newborn calves

on the pond
ducks and geese paddle
heads down, legs
freezing into ice
there's no food anyway
but some of them will make it

farmers gather in each others' shops
there's always an implement
getting fixed for summer
somewhere, someone
to talk to, laughter
what is a useless tool anyway?

they keep calm, heads down
watching their feet closely
sensible as those sturdy old brassieres
in 1950s magazines
white and pointed
at a sky of dreams
limited men
making do

salvage calf from downer cow

1.

the cows are coming for their grain
but the old cow isn't with them this time
  I find her far back in the pasture
  she takes a few steps, stops
  closes her eyes
hears the sound of pails and tries again

  she stops
  she closes her eyes
  waits several minutes
  makes it to the straw

2.

inside, cats are sleeping
the weather has turned stormy
and they know this
so they are tired
not pacing or worrying
or trying to sneak out the door
it is not a special day for them

in the pasture, the cow named Chubs
cannot get up
she is on a small patch of straw
face to the wind
needle snow pierces her eyes
a crow, the first one we've seen this spring
is sitting on her back

3.

the old cow's calf isn't ready to be born
but the vet tells us she can't live anymore
he suggests we shoot her
slice open her side
and go for the premature calf
before it dies too

no promises and no more time

surrounded by the storm
and this hard thing
it is difficult to believe in spring –
of sun warming calves
as they doze on the straw pack
but it is this memory
that moves us
to reach for life

4.

the other cattle circle
the dying cow
their eyes peering out of whiteness
the rifle shot stuns the air
and takes the old cow's grimace away

the big bull approaches, sniffing
bucking, around and around the body
steam escapes from the crude slash
the bull's bawling
is so angry, so disturbed
we've never heard him
make this sound before

5.

blowing snow and gusty winds
whirl up 50 maybe 60 crows
        every few minutes
I wonder how they know
about the dead cow so quickly

my son comes with the shot gun
but I touch his arm
I tell him about the simple beauty of skeletons
and how only scavengers
have stomachs for the transformation

    the cow lives
    in memory
    in the weak calf
    in the crows

fog covers her flanks in the morning
she lies, still dozing
Mescacakanis the coyote
trots among our farm animals

how peaceful she looks
as the sun quivers on the rim
beams revealing scarlet pastures
expansive fields, it pleases us
to say we own her

I watch her waking
    trying to feel detached
    trying not to feel the rush
of energy as day breaks
she waits for nothing, she
feeds on time, my
hours belong to her

there was a time when Indians
woke here in their summers, we
find their scrapers and hammerheads, she
is patient with our longings
and hides our generations
in the folds of her skirts
she will be here when rusting slabs
of steel remind others of us

the lazy looking mist
whispers the signal and disappears
coyote trots along
the stream and slips into
his day world

the sun's glare is upon us
they are one
the farm and the sun

the clatter of pails, the noise of machines
men lifting, struggling
growing old, children racing
growing up
breakfast, dinner, supper
the day roars over me

in the evening dust lingers in the sunset
tractor and cultivator scratch her broad back
that silhouette of dinosaur
grazing on the hills
if not the same

my friend and I walk the cow pasture
skipping pies, the smell of cow
pungent after steamy heat
I wonder what she's thinking
she's from town

the path is winding, deep in places
she wonders what willful dowager decided
this twist or that

a cow died in the meadow many years ago
the coyote has played with the white toys
and left them scattered, I wonder
what she thinks, still
she wants to see more
and we go on, cross the creek on dead trees
I show her how an infinitesimal insect
can kill a giant
and point to sawdust
at the centre of a tree trunk

I never noticed all this
before today

seeding time

I dream our combine see it coming
big and self-propelled across a field
swallowing a forgotten swath from last fall
fast coming so fast it begins to buck
the pick-up reaching into the sky then
catching dirt on its way down nearing
the hedge it doesn't stop or slow or veer
                              it punches
                              a hole
                    through five rows of trees
lurches through the yard my husband slumped at the wheel

the combine finally stops far out in another field
the one he's hell-bent to finish seeding if it kills him

the devil's breath, Saskatchewan, 1988

all day
the wind tries to convince me
I don't belong on this earth
it is trying to blow my memories away
along with the topsoil of our land
the wind is the devil's breath
wanting me to forget long manes of grass
and muskegs and sloughs, and mist
rising in the evenings
the wind blows dust in my eyes
and when I open them
I see tall poplars
broken along the empty creek
black spruce smaller than they were
pulling into themselves
trying to survive
the wind wants me to think
it will be like this forever

Roany's bones

on the meadow
in the pasture
the cow 's white bones are scattered again
I have piled those bones lovingly

the coyote has always been there before me
has strewn ribs and shoulder blades
and femurs across the open stretch

at night I hear him down there
his yapping pierces my sleep
I know what he's doing when it's quiet
he's trotting across the silver grass
carrying a bone in his mouth
shaking it
letting it fall
then he sits down and laughs
before he goes for another one

hog's head

the hog's head
long since severed from the hog's body
doesn't flinch as it is jostled
by living hooves
we've been out here for hours
trying again and again
to channel these pigs back into their pen

cold has crept into my feet
my back aches and I am covered with manure but
these pigs are our living
we can't give up
night falls on everything
my husband shouts out of the shadows
    here comes some more
    swing open the gate
I can still see the hog's head

it's dull eye fixed on the earth
feeling nothing
I on the other hand
know where I am

no time for mice

Robert Burns had time for mice
but I don't
the banker's leather shoe taps in town
I see the mice scamper on the combine's pick-up
wafted on the swath, racing
for the suicide edge
but the beast I ride is hungry and swift
and not paid for
we swallow them whole
and race on

bunny

six swathes left
I hear his heart pound
above the roar of the engine
he squats ahead of me
ears flat on his back at the last second he flees
        to the fifth swath
        fourth
        third
        second
he races into nowhere

string games

a small child plays the same game over and over —
she threads the ends of a string
through holes of a large button
knots them
and urges the button to the centre
then holding one end still
she winds a circle with her other hand
the button whirls, the string winds
around itself, around and around
her small fingers pull the looped ends
the string hums, elastic, travelling
back toward the button
tightening, letting go
the button whirls
the string hums and snaps
tiny fibres of cotton
beginning to break unnoticed, back and forth
over and under, humming and snapping

the kitchen is cluttered with tubs of yellow beans
picked days ago
the woman knows some will be showing
white fluffy mold
two cases of peaches sit on the cupboard, he
brought them home, lunch kits gape open
the supper table has been ravaged by hungry men
who ate and ran
a single light bulb dangles
bright on the table, shadows
mystify the corners of the room
where piles of bills
have mounted and fallen over

the child winds up the string again
feels the tension travel
through the twist to her knowing fingers

she relaxes the ends at the right second
her hands moving back and forth, the string
humming and snapping in and out
the button whirling
small threads breaking
beginning to be noticeable
the sound slightly different

the husband goes outside and the woman sits
staring at the button, hypnotized
by its orbit around the twirling string
there are escapes other women have taken
but she has been too strong too sane too good
    like the button
she whirls at the centre of his universe

    the man
comes back in the house, his shoulders
warn her of his fatigue
he has watered the cows but
has to rush back to the field, he wants her
to go out and feed them grain
with the five gallon pails
the ones that bang her legs
as she walks across the rough pens
    she says she will
and he goes out and comes back in five minutes
    is there coffee ready?
    and sandwiches for later?
he doesn't have time to fix the tractor wheel
it's shaking so badly
he thinks it might fall off
he goes out and comes back in again
looking for a flashlight
she is up this time so he will see she is working

the child winds up the string, the button whirls

and hums and snaps the child knows by the sound
it will soon break

the woman pulls on her old grey sweater
and goes outside
she hates feeding the cattle
she's afraid of the big bull
his long horns, the way he bucks
and swings his head at the pails
    in the darkness
she hears her husband starting the tractor
and wonders if he will get where he's going
without the wheel coming off
she fills the pails with chopped grain
struggles to crawl over the fence
holds the pails tight to her legs
and runs, hoping she won't fall

inside the farm house
where the light bulb glares
the child winds up the string, hears
it hum and snap hum and snap
the thin cotton threads breaking
the string getting finer at the centre
where it fits through the button holes
the child knows it will soon break
she can tell by the sound

sun in deep winter

sun shines on cold day, for some reason
a soft shine, reminiscent of April
old dog struggles to get up, decides to eat
as if she has to do it deliberately, as if
I have reminded her of life
sun streaks through the window
it's still a long time until spring
but yesterday I couldn't remember it at all

strange and still

there's something strange and still
about a warm winter afternoon
when the sun has dipped until
there is only a subtle peach haze on the clouds
and a silver sparkle on the trees
      the snow is soft
with endless rills and rolls
and tracks
birds hush up
for a change
and listen
animals smile with their gentle eyes
                  and people
people look and look
and take off their mitts
and adjust their hats
and try to keep it

I wonder if warm winter afternoons
mean this much everywhere
or just here

every year it gets stronger for me
the feeling that starts in April
when light is building
I want to keep it but
winter is everything here, it is
summer on the longest day
in the distance
I hear the roar of combines
gulping summer
winding into winter

unacceptable

beards of barley
bristle as a full moon
                        looms
the porcupine's belly
is soft and white tonight
and turned towards the sky
        no wind
and the temperature drops
        we wait
peering at the pale sheen of our crops
as darkness comes, but wait
        it might not freeze
        the wind could get up
        some clouds perhaps

in the morning
we chip ice off the wheat heads
squeeze kernels, wonder
        white frost
        black frost
        remember '79
by noon corn leaves droop
but still, out in the big fields

where the sun shines early
where the wind can manoeuvre
maybe

freedom

he is a World War II man
bomber pilot
silver-haired daddy redneck
in our kitchen
he spreads B-52 arms
flies again over the channel
to Berlin, cries
give me freedom
or let me die

in the living room his wife and I
laugh at a sit com
with a hand cupped furtively
over her mouth
she tells me in a low voice
how much she loves television
we don't have one at home –
he just hates TV
her eyes are happy
the thrill of
disobedience delicious
as a hard candy hidden in her mouth

universal pit

the man working in the hot gravel pit
both hands on levers, making
the caterpillar scrape and lift
cannot take his eyes off the job
but is peripherally aware
of a woman photographing wild flowers
on top of the high pit walls
her skirt whirling about her head
in a breeze he imagines cool

his T-shirt sticks to his hot back
each scoop of gravel gives way
to more gravel, at last
he can wait a moment for a late truck
he glances up to the ridge
but she is gone
and the truck is in sight
he puts his hat back on
noticing the foul dampness of the hat band
the motor puffs diesel breath at him
as he makes it work, hotter
than the sun's beady eye
that glares on his neck

the happiest man in town
strikes out on a bicycle
early

while the town is still sleeping
he poises himself at the stop sign
eyes excited, he
knows his territory
the hunt touches his nostrils
flared in the pale light, he
points his bike into the sun
the wheels go swish swish

he spots the first one
half a mile down the road
it glistens like a big diamond, he
knows from experience there will be more
perhaps on the other side
most often two or three
hit the ditch at once, if
it wasn't for him they might break
cut someone, start a fire
and they are valuable too
he only has to find them

when he returns to town
with his catch in the basket
people say *oh*
there he goes again

but the happiest man doesn't care
the chase will be there for him again tomorrow
while they drink coffee
and stare from murky windows

he is dressed casually
his shoes are smooth, tan, thin-soled
too fine for a small town in Saskatchewan
the folks know he must have bought them in Ottawa
maybe even Europe

the old cafe is gone and coffee row
is in the service station at the edge of town
the waitress flutters, doesn't know
what side to put his cup on
finally plops it down defiantly

he would like to sit with Charley
went to school with Charley
Charley was always the top dog

some of them saw the home town boy
at the banquet last night
chatting with the big shots at the head table
they point him out to each other on coffee row
it's been twenty years

yeah, I went to school with him
Charley nods in his direction
but doesn't look up
    hey
anybody know the price of flax this mornin'?

the home town boy busies himself
by soaking up the coffee in his saucer
with a napkin
his fine shoes under the table

a man dragging titles
anthropologist, historian, author
the weight of them tugs at his shoulders
along with camera, tape recorder
pages, ink

the forest is apprehensive at his coming
the trail is long, more
and more narrow, finally telescoping backwards
on a simple cabin
under its overhang an old man peers
pours hot water over tea
oh yes, the man dragging titles
is the neighbour's middle-aged son
the old man remembers

the cabin has not changed, only
the younger man recognizes the few belongings
as artifacts now, even the cutlery
a Hudson Bay axe stands in the corner
still attached to its handle
still in use

            the old man can't live much longer
        he's close to a hundred years old and
that he has existed on tea and biscuits
for the last thirty years is amazing
still, his mind is clear as ever, he

talks freely, doesn't get
that many chances, yes
he came to this area at the turn of the century
never had any schooling
was a scout for the police a long time ago
                    his life
enters the gadget, is caught there
the filaments of it winding

around and around
just what the man with titles wanted

the man dragging titles recourses the path
his tapes are full of another man's life
his titles are heavier than usual

the way out

two old people huddle
toes touching beneath blankets
her feet leap suddenly
at the touch of his sharp toenails
they try again
finally fit

the clock ticks
while cold squeezes the house
they hold on to each other

a full moon gapes through the window
they imagine it's an amber hole
stare until they see a place
outside the dome sky
they hold on to each other

so heavy and low

it is November in Saskatchewan   the sky so heavy and low
I can feel the weight of it on my chest   the days so short
and getting shorter   I can touch their sides
at midday